A TOOL
FOR CHRISTIANS

A book written to teach the use of Transactional Analysis
to those who care about growth in loving relationships
within the Christian community.

Jean C. Grigor

INTRODUCTION

WHY SHOULD CHRiSTIANS LEARN ABOUT TRANSACTIONAL ANALYSIS?

To those who would follow him, Jesus said:

"Do not judge others, so that God will not judge you, for God will judge you in the same way as you judge others, and he will apply to you the same rules you apply to others. Why then, do you look at the speck in your brother's eye, and pay no attention to the log in your own eye? How dare you say to your brother, 'Please let me take the speck out of your eye,' when you have a log in your own eye? You hypocrite! First take the log out of your own eye, and then you will be able to see clearly to take the speck out of your brother's eye."

(Matthew 7: 1 - 5)

For many Christians, T.A. is proving a most useful tool for removing logs, and most of us need all the help we can get!

A TOOL FOR CHRISTIANS

CONTENTS

CONTENTS

CHAPTER 1

YOU NEED TO KNOW YOU MATTER

The need for recognition

* You read a text like "Even the hairs of your head have all been counted" and you feel once again almost overwhelmed by how much you matter to your heavenly Father.

* One of the lads at the youth club has been saying very hurtful things to you recently, yet occasionally he seems to want to be as close as he was before. You are confused by this behaviour, but you decide to go on accepting him for himself, hoping that he will go on believing that he is of worth.

* An elderly widower lives alone and, one by one, his contemporaries die. He used to be cheery and outgoing, but neighbours say that the only time they see him now is when he shouts abuse at the children playing around his door.

What do these examples tell us about the human personality?

One of our most basic human needs is the need for recognition.

Each person needs to know he matters to somebody if he is to be a healthy, emotionally balanced personality, able to accept himself and to relate to others. And this need seems to go right back, to the very beginnings of our existence. Psalm 139 says this most beautifully, claiming that God's recognition of us goes right back to the time we were forming in the womb. Those who research into such matters tell us that we need loving human recognition right from that time too.

A well-cared-for baby is handled often and lovingly as she is fed, bathed, changed and caressed by her parents. In the way she is touched she gets the message of whether or not it is good for her to be alive — whether she is loved and valued, or unwanted and a nuisance to have around. (As she grows, she learns to accept recognition through facial expression, tone of voice, the spoken word — in fact, through any form of human communication).

1

Because the first form of recognition we receive as infants is given by touch, the technical term Transactional Analysis uses for a unit of recognition is a STROKE. Just as a father can comfort a crying child by stroking her head gently till she feels better, so in everyday relationships we can help people to feel loved and valued by giving psychological stroking.

Positive Strokes

What makes **you** feel as if you matter?

Each person is unique, and so each person could draw up a different list of positive strokes he values most.

One list might begin like this: a smile from a stranger, a word of encouragement when I'm feeling low, my sister admiring a new outfit, my boss saying "Well done. That must have taken a lot of time and thought", going for a walk with a good friend, Mum baking pancakes for tea, reading Romans chapter 8, having communion in a house church, a friend really listening to me (not just agreeing with my opinion).

Some strokes are meaningful, no matter how they come to us; some are of most value to us if they are given by someone we specially love or admire.

But, whatever the stroke, to be felt to be good it must be genuine. An insincere compliment has the opposite effect from a warm positive stroke. A genuine positive stroke invites us to feel more alive, more capable, more significant, more responsive to other people.

Transactional Analysis* is not "Christian". It is a theory of observable human behaviour and personality. It happens to be a theory which over and over again says some of what the New Testament says about human relationships. It is not a theology — it does not teach us about God; but many of its insights can be of value to the modern Christian working out how to love his neighbour as himself.

And so Christians will recognise the theory of Stroking. If a person receives positive stroking — in particular during his early childhood — he is likely to become a person who will give positive stroking to other people and to himself. The Scriptures say, "We love, because

*Transactional Analysis was originated by Dr. Eric Berne (1910-70) who was a practising psychiatrist in California, U.S.A.

2

He first loved us". The mark of being a loved child of God is that we love others. When Zacchaeus recieved loving recognition from Jesus, he was set free to love others more than he loved the money he had taken from them.

The Bible can be a rich source of positive stroking for us. Time and again, we are told that we are special, chosen, loved, redeemed, given gifts, set free. Even when we see our failures, our mistakes, our selfishness, our lack of love, it is within the context of forgiveness and renewal. The son might choose to squander his inheritance in the far country, but when he is sorry and returns he receives the father's hug, new clothes, a ring and a party! We are of immense value in the eyes of God. He gives each person unique recognition.

Negative strokes

Sometimes we recognise other people, not by building them up, but by putting them down. Negative strokes can diminish those who receive them. They can leave people feeling unhappy, anxious, less sure about themselves and their abilities, much less significant than they were before. Negative strokes are therefore words, looks, gestures and other behaviour which is unloving.

And each individual could make a list of the particular strokes she hates to receive and the ones he wishes he didn't give to other people. Being late for appointments, forgetting birthdays, passing on hurtful gossip, shouting someone down to cover up personal insecurity, getting even, blaming others... and so on.

No matter how greatly our parents loved us as children, we received both positive and negative stroking from them and from others, and so we learned to give both in our relationships. So great is our need for recognition from other people that, if we are not getting enough positive stroking, we will try to get negative strokes rather than be ignored — with no strokes at all.

Perhaps this is most easily seen in childhood. If children are being largely ignored while visitors are with their parents, it's common for them to begin to show off to get attention in spite of them knowing what might happen once the visitors go! Sometimes a child will pretend to be ill in order to get lots of special, anxious caring from his mother. This can be the start of a pattern of psychosomatic illness in adulthood.

Stroke Balance

A time of human crisis — for example, bereavement, redundancy, moving to a new district, adolescence, the arrival of a new baby, retirement — alters a person's normal stroke balance. Suddenly the strokes that came almost automatically are no longer there, and a person's whole emotional balance can be overthrown. He can behave quite differently from the person he seemed to be before the crisis — and often the behaviour is the symptom of the need for reassurance that he is still a person of worth in spite of what has happened.

Given time, most persons will restore themselves to near their original balance — but this can happen so much more quickly if people are surrounded by others who care. The adolescent might find a youth leader who seems to understand her; the new baby's mother might find a granny-substitute who will look after the baby for a while to give her time to devote special attention to the baby's two-year-old brother; the widow might find a church caring group to which she can belong without feeling the "odd-one-out" and where new friendships can develop.

There is also a balance unique to each person developed early in life between the positive and negative strokes he is used to receiving, and the positive and negative strokes he is used to giving to others. This tends to remain fairly constant unless something radical happens to change it. Sometimes this change can take place at conversion or through a good on-going human relationship. Such changes take place because a person who has previously experienced herself as of little worth to others discovers herself to be loved - and is set free to give as well as to receive love.

Becoming aware of the theory of stroking can certainly increase our consciousness of the benefit to others when we express to them the good thoughts and feelings we have towards them — thoughts and feelings that we often keep to ourselves. This can be a matter of will. We can choose to do it.

Learning a theory of human behaviour can show a Christian with some precision what areas of his life could be changed or enhanced. The theory of T.A. also shows what to do in order to change behaviour. Where our faith comes in is that we believe that change in the attitude of our human hearts and change in the behaviour that springs from those attitudes is the work of the Holy Spirit.

"The Spirit produces love, joy, peace, patience, kindness, goodness, faithfulness, humility, and self-control. . .
The spirit has given us life; he must also control our lives."

(Gal. 5:22, 25.)

Throughout the centuries Christians have known to ask for what they want in prayer.

"Bad as you are, you know how to give good things to your children.
How much more, then, will the Father in heaven give the Holy Spirit to those who ask Him!"

(Luke 11: 13.)

Many of us, especially as young Christians, have prayed earnestly, over and over again, words like "O God, make me more loving, please!" What we have failed to see the need to do, is to be far more specific — not that **God** needs more specific instructions, but that **we** need to work out step by step what being more loving will entail. Sometimes the Holy Spirit does suddenly infuse our hearts with a glow of love for a particular person, making it easy to say and do loving things to him. Far more often our Heavenly Father allows the discipline of working at what we need to improve.

Bert had a bad relationship at work. He didn't really understand how it had developed that way. Each day he prayed that it would become better, and each day he acted as if the bad feelings could be ignored, managing to keep himself from saying hurtful things and trying not to feel hurt by the other. But the bad feelings persisted inside both parties. Eventually he realised that he could reach out to his workmate with a loving gesture — a positive stroke. He had to work out carefully which stroke might be understood and acceptable to the other person as a warm offer of friendship.

He had to take the risk of being rejected and his gesture misinterpreted. So he put love into action although he was not feeling any great love in his heart at that time. His workmate responded and accepted his offer. Gradually, over a few weeks that situation improved radically between them and the warmth they had once felt for each other came back.

A positive stroke given is merely an invitation to another to feel loved and accepted and valued. The invitation can be turned down.

In the same way, a negative stroke is merely an invitation to feel hurt, or rejected, or worthless. It is possible to attempt to understand why another person is dealing out negative strokes and to come to the conclusion that she is doing so because she is not feeling too good, and that the last thing she really needs is for you to feel the same and reject her. It's possible **not** to accept the invitation offered through the gift of a negative stroke!

Self stroking

Jesus commanded us to love our neighbours as ourselves. What does it mean to "love ourselves?" Putting this alongside other texts from Scripture we can safely come to the conclusion that it does not mean "indulge yourself", "always put yourself first", or "do exactly whatever you happen to feel like doing".

Joan was feeling dreadful. Somehow, everything had gone wrong since she burned the porridge at breakfast. One thing after another had led to her having a thumping headache. In two hours the family would be home demanding food and attention. Joan had the choice of going on feeling miserable and of probably spreading her misery through the family as they arrived home, or of doing something about loving herself. She decided to give herself the kind of attention that would help her feel better.

She ran a warm, perfumed bath, turned on one of her favourite records of light romantic music, and relaxed. Later, over a cup of coffee; she decided on a menu for the evening meal that was both easy for her and popular with the family. Her self-stroking was effective. She knew that by the happiness around the table that evening.

At a more serious level, than was Joan's bad mood, is the behaviour some Christians indulge in, sometimes severely damaging their own health and the relationships in their families. These are the people who, from the very worthy motive of serving the Lord with zeal, forget that there are limits to the strains they can put on their minds, bodies . . . and families. Sometimes children of keen Christians grow up feeling unloved and unwanted because their parents put everything else before them. The spouses of the "pillars of the church" can feel exploited, used and neglected. All too often keen Christians confuse loving themselves with self-indulgence, and so seriously abuse themselves that they suffer breakdowns in emotional and physical health. Jesus pointed to a balance in loving our neighbours as ourselves.

Love has to be experienced before it can be passed on. Are you receiving love? Are you loving yourself? Are you working on loving other people appropriately?

---

1. *Luke 15 : 11-24.*

For you to think through by yourself, or with others.

1. Which words from the Bible give you a special positive stroke when you read them?

2. Look up the Parable of the Prodigal Son (Luke 15) and note all the positive strokes given in it — and all the negative ones!

3. If you were responsible for a service of worship in your local congregation or group, how could you use this concept of stroking in it?

4. Think of a particular person you know who is needing a lot more positive stroking than he or she is receiving right now.

   a) what kind of stroking would likely to be meaningful for him or her? (e.g. physical touch giving her a gift, telling him something good about his personality...)

   b) think of a positive stroke you could give that person and make a contract in a group, or with a friend, that you will give it.

5. Imagine an old widow now living alone in your locality. What strokes will she no longer have that she would once be used to? How could a local congregation give this lady some positive stroking?

6. When you feel out-of-sorts what could you do to make yourself feel better so that you could be more loving to those around you?

Suggestions for using stroking in small group worship.

a) Ask the group to stand in a circle holding hands and say the Benediction together.

b) If the group is sitting in a circle, ask each to place their right hand on the shoulder of the person on their right and pray silently for that person. After a short silence, the leader can finish with "Amen".

c) Share in twos a few details about a situation likely to be a difficulty in the coming week. After the sharing, the pair can hold hands or place their right hand on each other's shoulder, and pray silently for strength for their partner in the coming week.

7

CHAPTER 2

WHAT MAKES PEOPLE TICK?

Ego states.

*   On one committee of your church there is a man who seems to object to everything that might bring about much-needed change. He is so destructive in his comments that some other keen members have handed in their resignations.

*   Yesterday Margot was amazed at how much her moods varied within the brief space of an hour. She had been feeling tired, and was relaxing with a cup of coffee when she heard a child screaming. Without a thought of her tiredness, she rushed out, rescued a toddler from an over-playful dog, carried him to his mother, then sat listening to her as she shared her loneliness in coming to a new district. Within the hour she was back home 'phoning around the neighbours to arrange a get-together for the young mother. Her husband arrived home to the sound of her singing as she prepared the evening meal.

What goes on inside our personalities that we can think, feel and act so differently in differing situations? What makes people tick? This is a question thinking people have asked for centuries, and each theory of human personality uses its own terminology to explain what goes on within us and why. Transactional Analysis proposes an apparently simple explanation of why we behave as we do. Eric Berne suggested that just as the human body has physical organs each with special functions, we could imagine that each personality also had 'psychic organs' which were the source of feelings, thoughts and behaviour. He called these EGO STATES and named three — the Parent, the Adult and the Child. To represent this there is a simple three circle diagram. (Diag. 1)

1. *Diagram of the human personality.*

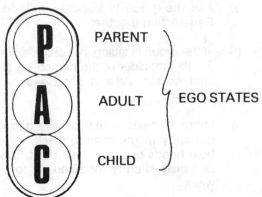

PARENT

ADULT   EGO STATES

CHILD

A little child is primarily concerned with his own needs, wants and feelings, and behaves in a way aimed at expressing them and having them satisfied. Whether he likes it or not, each person as he grows up retains within himself the child he once was. And so one part of our personality is called "CHILD". When a grown-up feels like dancing for joy, bursts into tears, stamps angrily out of a meeting, praises God with his whole heart, manipulates others to get his own way, drives recklessly or feels sorry for himself because he has 'flu, that grown-up person is in his Child ego state.

When a human infant is totally dependent on her parents, the only part of her personality available to her is her Child; but very soon that little girl will begin to take a share in looking after herself. Listen to a toddler playing. Watch her as she approaches the heater and says, "Don't touch! Too hot!", then looks up for her mother's approval. Watch her as she tries to force a biscuit into her dolly's mouth and says, "Be a good girl and eat it all up". That little girl's "PARENT" ego state is developing.

The Parent ego state is that part of us that looks after the Child within us and the Child within others. Gradually during childhood and adolescence a person's natural parents hand over their role to the growing person until she becomes independent — able to "parent" herself and others.

To make it easier to observe which behaviours fit into each ego state, the Parent and Child ego states are sometimes diagrammed as sub-divided. The divisions of the Parent are the NURTURING PARENT, and the CRITICAL PARENT. (Diag. 2)

2. *Diagram showing sub divisions of Parent and Child Ego States.*

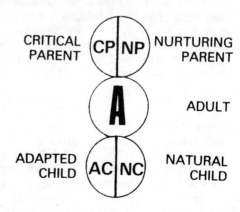

CRITICAL PARENT

NURTURING PARENT

ADULT

ADAPTED CHILD

NATURAL CHILD

9

Just as a good parent gives his child lots of loving care and attention, sets standards and boundaries on behaviour for the child's safety (social as well as physical) and reprimands the child when she breaks his rules, so, when the little girl grows up, her Parent ego state continues to function in this way for her and for others. When a man puts a loving arm around the shoulders of a colleague who has received bad news, when a student draws up a protest petition against unfair treatment meted out to a fellow student, when a woman criticises a neighbour for her dog's behaviour, when someone is so scared of losing his authority that he defensively rejects everything new committee members suggest, then these people are acting from their Parent ego state and looking after themselves or others. Unfortunately, when a person's Parent is looking after the interests of his internal Child without trying at the same time to consider the interests of the Child ego states of others, the Parent often acts unwisely, unnecessarily over-indulging or hurting himself and others.

"Do for others", Jesus said, "just what you want them to do for you". And "Love your neighbour. . . as yourself". If you do this by looking after your neighbour without looking after yourself, you can bring yourself to the point of breakdown, whereas if you look after yourself and not your neighbour you will soon find yourself cut off from meaningful relationships.

The third ego state is called the "ADULT". A little child can think things through for himself, but because he hasn't much experience of life and cannot cope adequately with conceptual thinking, he will often arrive at a conclusion no adult would. The part of the personality that can handle ideas, come to conclusions, weigh up facts, act on decisions, assess probabilities, compute, compile — the part which can think rationally and objectively in the here-and-now, is called the Adult. In many ways it can be a misleading term because in everyday life we use the word "adult" to mean mature or grown-up whereas, in Transactional Analysis, "Adult" used to denote the ego state does not have that exact meaning.

If we know all the facts and think them through objectively in a situation, we are using the Adult ego state. So, when a boy counts up his pocket money to see if he can afford a new football and reckons he will have to wash his father's car once again to have the right amount, he is using his Adult. When a Halls' Convener receives applications from three different organisations for accommodation in the church premises all asking for the same evening and he 'phones up the person in charge of each to enquire into the needs and number of each one and then allocates on the basis of information received, he is using his Adult.

There are two main styles of behaviour shown by the Child ego state, and these are labelled NATURAL CHILD and ADAPTED CHILD. (Diag. 2) When a person is in Natural Child, he or she reacts spontaneously and freely expresses whatever is being felt, whether that is fear, sorrow, joy, anger or whichever emotion appropriately fits that situation. An example of this in John's Gospel is in the story of Jesus weeping at the tomb of his friend Lazarus. This may well be embarrassing for others who think emotions should not be expressed publicly.

Most of us are trained from early childhood, by example and by advice, to keep our emotions under control — to put a face on things, not to let people see how we are really feeling. When we do this, we behave in a manner adapted to suit what we imagine are other people's expectations. This is called being in the Adapted Child. When a loved one dies some mourners, especially some Christian people, try to appear as if they were not hurt, bewildered, sad or angry. If someone says something which offends us, instead of being open and expressing how we feel and finding out why they said what they did, we withdraw to lick our wounds in private and end up with resentment towards that person, which can destroy the relationship far more than the original statement.

Because we think we might make a fool of ourselves if we speak out in a group, we keep quiet and deny the others the benefit of our contribution. Because we imagine we or other people cannot cope with new forms or worship, new ways of discovering depths of Christian community, we react from our Adapted Child and call them ''dangerous''. Adapted Child behaviour tends to be the opposite of the child-like faith that takes risks and makes new and exciting discoveries.

A mature and well-balanced personality is able to feel, think and act appropriately in a situation, whether it calls for her being in the Child, Parent or Adult ego state(s). No one ego state is more " the real person" than any other. Each person needs all ego states ready and able to function. Her energy flows freely amongst them all, and she can choose to use them separately or together.

In ethical decision-making, for instance, all three ego states are used. The Adult gathers all the facts available. The facts include the needs and feeling of the Child as the result of life's experiences, together with all the Parent has stored up from past teaching of parents and other authority figures. These are considered alongside estimations of probable outcomes of several possible ways of behaving, and only then is the decision made about what is the truly loving thing to do in the given situation. A reaction based solely on what an individual wants (Child) or on what he thinks he ought to do because this is what he was taught to do (Parent) can be an irresponsible way of handling a situation.

Those familiar with the Gospels may find it helpful to have examples of the various ego states highlighted from these records.

"I assure you," said Jesus in Matthew 18:3, "that unless you change and become like children, you will never enter the Kingdom of heaven." He also said, "Your Father already knows what you need before you ask him." (Matt. 6:8), and in the following verse, "This, then, is how you should pray: 'Our Father in heaven. . .'"

As in many other places he urges the use of the Child ego state as a source for our behaviour.

Often, through parables, Jesus urges us to be people who think through the consequences of our actions and to weight up facts — to be in the Adult ego state. This is so in Luke 14: 28-33, where he talks of the cost of being His disciple, and in the parable of the pounds (Luke 19:23) where he rebukes the servant who did not think logically what he could do with the money he had been given.

Into the Parent ego state of his followers, Jesus placed many values and standards by which they were to judge their own thoughts and actions, and also to assess the actions of others. "Love your enemies." . . . "Pray for those who persecute you." . . . "Take heed that no one leads you astray." His direct command to Peter to "Feed my sheep" has encouraged many of his people throughout the ages to look after others.

A knowledge of the theory about ego states provides a tool for more successful handling of relationships — including a person's relationship with God. It can help us diagnose how we are coming across to others and how they are reacting to us. It can help us understand why we sometimes behave as we do.

If the terms "Parent", "Adult" and "Child" as used in Trans-actional Analysis become part of the shared language of a couple or a group, the theory can help them towards more satisfactory ways of relating to each other.

Old destructive patterns of relating and behaving can be changed as awareness of them emerges. The resources to be found in the Christian life of forgiveness and reconciliation in relationship with

12

God and the Christian community can enable and support change, so that we can grow in loving. Love doesn't just happen.

For you to think through by yourself, or with others.

First, to help you begin to be able to diagnose ego states:—

A. Think of a group you belong to.

   1) Recall three incidents in the group — one where its members were in their Child ego states, one for the Adult ego states, and one where the group was interacting Parent to Parent, or Parent to Child.

   2) Which ego state seems to dominate when your group comes together?

B. Think of three incidents or situations last week — one each for when you were in your Child, your Parent, and your Adult.

C. How differently might you pray if you were in your Child ego state, or your Adult, or your Parent?

D. In a small group Bible Study, choose a well-known parable of Jesus with various characters portrayed in it. Discuss which ego states you see as the plot unfolds.

E. Which words of Jesus most appeals to your
   i)   Standard-setting Parent?
   ii) Nurturing Parent?
   iii) Critical Parent?
   iv) Adult?
   v)   Child when you are happy?
   vi) Child when you feel insecure?

Then, to help you apply your ability to spot ego states:—

1. How can various parts of a service of worship tune in to all three ego states of the worshippers? Which is your usual ego state for Sunday morning?

2. Think of a person you know who sometimes needs your help. Write down two things you could do for the person which would

13

be truly nurturing, and two things which would be over-nurturing and tend to take away the person's dignity and independence.

3. Write down the names or initials of three people you dislike or avoid. Under each name write five words to describe their personalities as they come across to you.

Now compare the three lists. Can you see any similarities in your way of classifying people you dislike? Has this exercise put you in touch with a prejudice you might hold against certain types of people — e.g. people in authority, people older/younger than you, people of a different sex, people who remind you of someone else, etc.?

Do you need to change some of the content of your Critical Parent? If so, use your Adult to figure out the difference between your prejudice against certain people, and reality.

CHAPTER 3

DO YOU EVER TALK TO YOURSELF?

Internal Dialogue and Internal Conference

Have you ever noticed yourself slipping into an old, familiar but unhelpful pattern of behaviour — one you've kept since early childhood?

It could be
> "I'll never be any good, no matter how hard I try. No use asking me".

or
> "Just call me 'The Willing Horse'. History repeats itself — no-one else will do it, so 'muggins' takes it on. Why is it always left to me?"

or
> "I can't give up. Who would take over if I left? Other people are inexperienced and would mess things up. I'm indispensable".

If so — what can you do about it?

In order to understand the terms "INTERNAL DIALOGUE" and "INTERNAL CONFERENCE", it is necessary to have understood the term "Ego state" and the particular meaning Transactional Analysis gives to the words used for the three ego states, namely, "Parent", "Adult" and "Child".

Inside all people at all times there are available three distinct ways of feeling, thinking and acting — the three ego states: three ways of expressing the human personality. In any given situation, a person chooses, consciously or unconsciously, to feel, think or act in any one ego state, or sometimes in a combination or sequence of ego states. It is quite normal, though not always wise, for a person to react to a given situation in much the same way as she learned to react to similar ones in childhood.

15

Imagine that someone has done something he now regrets. He will probably tell his friends, "I didn't think. I did it automatically!" or "I went to that meeting really determined to hold my tongue no matter what she said, but, when it came to the bit, I just blew my top".

These are both examples of the Internal Dialogue at work where, for good relationships to exist, the Internal Conference would have been much more appropriate.

The Internal Dialogue is the interaction within a person that goes on between his Parent and his Child ego states. THE ADULT IS BY-PASSED.

3. *In the Internal Dialogue, the Adult Ego State is by-passed.*

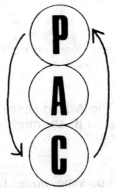

The function of the Parent is to nurture or criticise the Child; to give parenting to the Child within. The Parent ego state reacts to whatever is going on in the Child ego state. In some people, if the Child feels hurt, the Parent swings in with whatever will provide comfort for the hurt inner Child at that moment, and, at the same time, it springs to attack the source of the hurt to provide a security against further hurt. On the other hand, there are people whose Parent reacts quite differently. For those people, their experience of parenting when young was not of being protected so much as of being under attack. No matter what they did, their parents were never completely satisfied. Although now physically grown-up, their Parent ego state continues to be over-critical.

Let me illustrate both types of Internal Dialogue. Imagine someone with an overweight problem. She goes regularly to a Slimmers' Club. She is quite a shy person, and always avoids confrontation if at all possible. One day, Mrs. Smith, one of the Committee members at the Slimmers' Club, says something which hurts her. She says nothing in reply, but her inner Child immediately withdraws to lick the wounds.

On her way home, she meets a friendly neighbour and she agrees to have a cup of coffee with her. Into the coffee she puts two spoonfuls of sugar, and her Nurturing Parent even allows her to feel quite justified in enjoying a chocolate biscuit! Eventually she confides in her friend the hurtful thing Mrs. Smith said to her at the club, and gets a lot of satisfaction from hearing the friend cap her story with another one that she has heard about the same person. The inner Parent has comforted the hurt Child, and also attacked the source of the hurt, thereby providing an effective way of passing on the Internal Dialogue through the whole community!

As a result of the hurt woman using only two of the ego states available to her in this situation, she acted in a way which further harmed herself (overeating) and perpetuated damaged relationships.

The Internal Conference is the interaction within a person which goes on among all three ego states, with the Adult acting as Executive. The Adult takes account of all the Child feelings and all the Parent opinions and reactions, and weighs these up with all the other available data at its command, especially the probable consequences of certain words or actions, and their appropriateness to this particular situation. (Diag. 4)

4. *The Internal
Conference—
all Ego States
involved.*

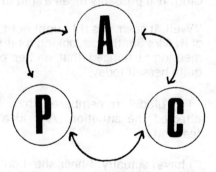

Continuing with the above example, imagine how it might have been, had the woman brought in her Adult ego state and held an Internal Conference.

Child: "Ouch! That hurt me. I feel like crying, but I'm not going to let her see she hurt me".

Parent: "I don't deserve that kind of treatment! In fact, I deserve a nice chocolate biscuit, just like mum used to give me when I was young if I had been hurt".

17

Adult:	"Hey, wait a minute! I know I'm feeling terrible, but is it really going to help to have a biscuit?"
Parent:	"And I have been so good about my diet recently".
Adult:	"Let's look at this objectively for a change. What's going to happen next week at the Club if I've put on weight? A fine! That's going to hurt too!"
Child:	"Well, I suppose so, but I'm still feeling sore".
Parent:	"Mrs Smith ought to be punished for saying that to me in front of all those folk".
Child:	"Hey, if I tell my friend all about it, she'll probably spread it round, and in the end they'll all be on my side against her!"
Parent:	"Good idea! That'll teach her a thing or two".
Adult:	"I've been thinking. In the long run, what's all this going to achieve? Certainly, if I spread gossip about that woman she'll be one person less for me to have as a friend in the Club. It'll probably mean a split in the Club too".
Parent:	"Well, it seems as if I ought not to do that. Come to think of it, Mrs Smith was looking a bit tired and strained at the meeting. I noticed that earlier on. Perhaps she wasn't quite herself today".
Adult:	"I'm glad I remembered that. It could certainly have affected the situation. Any idea how I could help her feel better?"
Parent:	"I have, actually. I hear she didn't get a holiday this year and her baby has been crying a lot in the middle of the night. What about me 'phoning her up and suggesting I take the baby off her hands for a few hours tomorrow?"
Child:	"That would be great! I like babies, especially when I can give them back to their mothers again! I've been a bit lonely this past while with all my kids off my hands now".
Adult:	"That's a good all-round solution. Where's the telephone directory?"

By way of contrast to the above situation, imagine a parish minister. He had been a very sensitive little boy who always tried to please, but, somehow or other, he never seemed to be able completely to satisfy his parents. He had a brother and sister not much younger than himself and, as he was the eldest, was expected to take responsibility for them much of the time. He loved doing this and would spend hours playing with them until his father found him and criticised him for "frittering away his time when he ought to be working at his lessons". He would get his books out and be engrossed in them when his mother would discover him and he would be scolded for not keeping the younger ones out of mischief.

He loved the parish ministry, but sometimes when he was out visiting his parishioners he found himself wondering if he had done enough study that week to prepare himself for Bible Class; and, when he was thoroughly enjoying some stimulating reading, he would start getting a nagging feeling that he really ought to be out seeing old Mrs. Brown instead. He tried hard to keep a good balance of visiting and studying in his ministry. He used his Adult to arbitrate between what his Child enjoyed and what his Parent told him he ought to do, and generally, he coped quite well.

One week he had spent a particularly long time in his study preparing for a weekend conference with his elders. Not without some anxiety, he had made the decision that this took priority over routine visits that week. In fact, he had asked his wife on Friday morning in the last-minute rush not to disturb him unless in an emergency. At tea-time that evening, just before he left for the conference, she told him, "By the way, Mrs. Murray 'phoned this morning when you were busy to say that her mother hadn't been too well this week. I said you'd pop in on your rounds next week".

Later on that evening, he arrived at the conference centre well prepared for the weekend's work. A small group of older members were obviously talking about him, from the silence which fell when he entered.

"Mr. Murray sends his apologies. You've heard about his mother-in-law, of course", one of them volunteered.

"My wife took a 'phone call this morning. She hasn't been too well this week, I hear. I must visit her on Monday", he replied.

"Cerebral haemorrhage, the Doctor said. She's in a coma. They say she'll not last the night, so I doubt you'll be a bit late on Monday! It's a pity you couldn't have managed this morning. She took it about 2 o'clock in the afternoon. One of your most faithful members, too."

19

The rest of the elders arrived, and the conference began, but it never got off the ground. The minister got through the first session, but couldn't really concentrate. He didn't sleep a wink that night, and the next morning he was sure he had 'flu. He handed his papers over to the Session Clerk and went home, quite sick with guilt.

From an external source he had experienced a Critical Parent rebuke. His Child had responded immediately with guilt feelings. His internal Critical Parent had joined forces with the external Critical Parent, to condemn, so there was no hope for him. He felt he deserved the criticism. He felt completely guilty. He was so buried under this deluge of guilty feelings that his Adult might as well have been decommissioned — he didn't even attempt to use it. The only way he felt (unconsciously) he could cope was to become sick.

At first, this theory might seem highly introspective. It might seem that, were a person to stop and analyse everything he was about to do and say, he would never get on with the business of living.

The fact is that a person can begin to identify quite quickly when he is in the Internal Dialogue situation instead of the Internal Conference, and he can do this with practice by becoming aware of his feelings. It's a bit like being the pilot of a small 'plane in control of where he wants to go, and suddenly finding that instead of being at the plane's controls he is sitting helplessly on a see-saw, going up and down and not getting anywhere.

Everyone has her own Adapted Child reactions. These are old familiar feelings and behaviour patterns to which individuals return self-indulgently again and again. They begin as a result of childhood experiences and are traceable throughout life. A little person figures out how to cope with a certain inner feeling, and no matter how uncomfortable or destructive that feeling is, she will return to it again and again because it fits in with the way she sees herself and the rest of the world.

From the previous illustration, the slimmer's Adapted Child reaction was a kind of righteous indignation at a hurt, which she used to justify gossip and to attempt to prove that she was innocent. The minister's reaction was guilt, the feeling that no matter how hard he tried he'd probably not do the right thing by others — which he used eventually to stop himself doing anything but feeling guilty and sick that week-end.

When a person can identify which particular see-saw he jumps onto, it becomes increasingly easy to sense the old pattern of behaviour, stop it quickly, and get behind the controls of the 'plane again. Some old feelings tend more towards damaging relationships with others, while others seem to affect a person's inner feelings concerning his ability to function as he wants to.

It sounds as if even St. Paul sometimes found himself on the see-saw! "I don't do the good I want to do; instead I do the evil that I do not want to do." (Romans 7:19)

When a person realises that his automatic reaction in any given situation is not the most appropriate for building healthy, loving relationships, he can sit down with himself and use his Adult to data-process the contents of his Child, his Parent and all the other relevant information about the reality of the situation he is in, till he comes to a decision about which is the loving way — then he can act appropriately.

Sometimes it's a lot easier to identify and stop these feelings and behaviour patterns if someone else helps. This is another place where a caring community can be confronting, strengthening and healing. These reactions are just so familiar to each person — it feels so normal to be on that particular see-saw — that it often requires another person's gentle reminder to get the Adult functioning again, so he can move on.

"Love never gives up. Its hope, faith and patience never fail. It is love, then, that you should strive for". (1 Corinthians, chapters 13 & 14)

For you to think through by yourself, or with others.

WORKSHEET : "THE INTERNAL CONFERENCE"

When a person has difficulty in changing an old pattern of behaviour, making a decision, or solving a problem, it can be that he is caught between his internal Parent and Child ego states and is not using the Adult ego state's executive powers.

21

If one of the above applies to you, complete this worksheet.

1. In this box, write all that your Parent is telling you about this problem.

```



```

    ie a) What have you been taught concerning this by your actual parents, other authority figures?
    b) What does the Bible say about it?
    c) What other sayings or proverbs are in your mind concerning it?
    d) Any other "don't, ought, should, must, never, always" statements?
    e) What would keep you safe? What would keep others safe?

2. In the next box, write down all that your Child is telling you about this problem.

```



```

ie a) Describe each feeling you get around this subject.

b) What are your wants, your needs, your desires, your likes and dislikes concerning it?

c) What does your Child suspect might happen to you?

d) What 'magic' solution would you wish for?

3. Now, in the final box, put all the objective Adult facts you can think of about the situation.

ie a) Describe the cold facts about the problem as if it belonged to someone else.

b) Now in one short sentence define the problem clearly.

c) Now look through all you have written in the Parent and Child boxes and put a tick beside those factors you consider it reasonable still to influence a person of your age and circumstances. Delete the remainder.

d) Next, list every possible solution you can think of.

e) Do any of these solutions seem feasible, taking into consideration the content of your Parent and Child ego states?

f) If not, list your reasons for rejecting them.

g) Are your reasons valid, or are they really excuses you have used on other occasions?

h) Choose one solution, and try it out.

i) If you think you have found a solution but are not completely certain, check it out with someone whose judgment you respect who will be likely to support you in any new behaviour pattern you might wish to begin. If that person thinks your solution is wise, list the steps you will need to take to get where you want to go, then contract with him to carry out the new behaviour.

j) If you have found no possible solution, ask yourself: "Why do I need to believe this problem is impossible to solve?".

CHAPTER 4

AND WHAT ABOUT TALKING TO OTHERS?

Transactions

* Do you ever have the feeling that you could go on sharing with a friend for hours because you are exactly on the same wave-length?

* One of your neighbours is a middle-aged woman who recently nursed her authoritarian father until he died, leaving her alone. Since then she seems to have been seeking you out, and always with some small problem, and the words, "Oh dear. What should I do?"

* Do you ever have an uneasy feeling that someone is manipulating you in the way he carries out his side of the conversation?

Since the days of the early church Christians have been fighting amongst each other, and feeling guilty that we are not better able to "live at peace with everybody" as instructed in Romans 12 v. 18. We seem also to have a lot of difficulty when it comes to carrying out the word in the epistles about confronting each other in love. . . "My brothers, if someone is caught in any kind of wrongdoing, those of you who are spiritual should set him right; but you must do it in a gentle way. And keep an eye on yourselves, so that you will not be tempted too." (Gal. 6:1)

There are some gracious individuals who seem to be natural peace makers, or who without training apart from their growth in grace, can find the right word to say to bring peace and love back into relationships. The rest of us, however, could do with some help and training in this very important area.

The term "Transactional Analysis", as well as being the name for the whole theory of human personality, is also more specifically used for looking at what goes on in the transactions between one

25

individual and another. If one person communicates either with or without words to another and the other replies, then a TRANS-ACTION has taken place in communication. Since relationships are made up of countless transactions, day in and day out, it is necessary to have some tool for examining some of those transactions to see what is going wrong if a relationship is not good, or to see what could be even better if a relationship can be enhanced.

The tool used is the ability to spot ego states. When two people have a conversation there are potentially six ego states for the words and gestures to come from and to go to. My Parent ego state can talk to your Parent, or your Child, or your Adult. You can choose whether to respond to me from your Parent, your Child or your Adult.

5. *A conversation between you and me could include any ego state in me addressing any ego state in you - and so could your replies.*

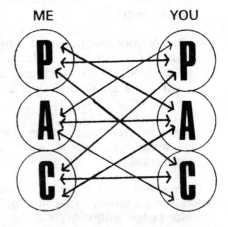

ME   YOU

Two church members are chatting together in the hall before the morning service. Brian looks at his watch, and says matter-of-factly from his Adult, "It's two minutes to eleven." Pat could reply from any of her ego states, depending on how she is feeling, the impression she wants to convey to Brian, her past experiences of similar situations, and so on. She might respond from her Adult, "It's time we went into church." She might fly into a Child panic, put her hand over her mouth, say, "Oh no, and I've still to see to the nursery chairs before the service, and there I go, late again. . ." On the other hand Pat might turn on a very patronising Parent ego state, and reply, "Of course, my dear. I've been keeping you back with all my problems. You'll want to get into the service on time. You run along." The reply Pat has given to Brian will have called out a response in him. If she has given the Adult reply to his Adult statement, they will both go into church without any hang-over from that part of their conversation. If the reply has come from Pat's Child, Brian will probably have switched to his Parent ego state, and

26

either be saying to himself, "Oh, really! It's high time Pat learned to be more responsible about her time keeping!" or "Perhaps I ought to have offered to go and help her put out the chairs." If, on the other hand, Pat had come on with the patronising Parent, Brian might well have swung into his Child ego state and have felt extremely put down and manipulated.

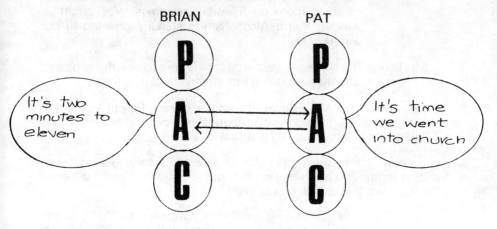

6. *An Adult to Adult Complementary Transaction.*

T.A. identifies three main types of transactions as people talk together and names them COMPLEMENTARY, CROSSED and ULTERIOR.

In a Complementary transaction, the stimulus given from a specific ego state seeks a response from the corresponding appropriate ego state, and the response comes from the appropriate one. The Complementary transaction in the above conversation would have been the Adult to Adult one. . . . "It's two minutes to eleven." . . . "It's time we went into church." (Diag. 6) If someone is feeling very sorry for himself because he is not well, then from his Child he will give out some message, verbal or non-verbal, that he is looking for a caring Parent ego state to look after him. If he gets it, a Complementary transaction has taken place.

Complementary transactions keep life running smoothly as people get what they want and expect in communication, although this way of operating can sometimes be a bit dull, and might mean that some people are keeping the peace because they are afraid of confrontation, not that everything is necessarily as good as the lack of fighting would seem to indicate.

Church people are often very fond of being in the Parent ego state. Here is a snatch of typical complementary Parent-Parent conversation before a church committee meeting:

Mr. Smith: Among the correspondence tonight there'll be a letter from the local AA branch asking if they can use the meeting room on Tuesday evenings. We ought to support them. Alcoholism is steadily growing in our community.

Mr. Brown: It's the least we can do, really. It's a dreadful problem, and they are doing something about it, after all.

Mr. Smith and Mr. Brown are agreed. Their Parent ego states could go on talking to each other about this topic and agreeing, and in fact at the meeting they do just that.

However, at the meeting is Mrs. Blue. Her Parent ego state is very willing to join the conversation too, but it contains quite a different point of view to those of the two men.

Mrs. Blue: I've been sitting here listening to Mr. Brown supporting Mr. Smith's ideas, but all I can say is that **they** haven't got daughters who might come under the influence of the unsavoury characters that might begin to hang around our premises if we allow them to use our meeting room. Of course these poor drunkards should be given help, but after all they have themselves to blame for the state they have sunk to, and we must protect the young and innocent God has given into our care. Have Mr. Brown and Mr. Smith forgotten that Tuesday nights are Brownie nights?

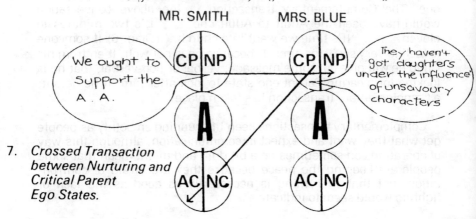

MR. SMITH — We ought to Support the A.A. — CP NP / A / AC NC

MRS. BLUE — CP NP / A / AC NC — They haven't got daughters under the influence of unsavoury characters

7. *Crossed Transaction between Nurturing and Critical Parent Ego States.*

Mrs. Blue sat down after a final glare at the two men concerned, and the majority of the people at the meeting who had been feeling comfortable at the conversation between Mr. Smith and Mr. Brown, now feels decidedly uncomfortable. For a moment, nobody speaks. Then Mrs. Black rises to her feet.

"If I remember correctly," she begins quietly, "the letter asked for the use of the meeting room at 7.30 and the Brownies go off home around 6.30. I don't know much about the AA, but I think the people in that organisation would be people who would be making every effort to help each other to act responsibly.

"I suggest that we give them the chance to meet in our room, and at the same time let them know that the Brownies meet earlier in our premises, so that they can take any precautions they might feel to be necessary. We could also tell the Brownie leader of our decision so she can make sure the Brownies go off home when their meeting is finished."

What kind of transactions were going on at that meeting? If Mr. Smith and Mr. Brown had been able, through the strength of their Nurturing Parent ego state convictions, to make sure everyone else would feel the same, there would have been no unpleasantness, but something else was going on inside Mrs. Blue. Somehow a very sensitive spot had been touched insider her (perhaps she had someone in her family with a drink problem in the past and had been scared or ashamed of it?), and whatever that was, her reaction was to leap into her Critical Parent and try to make Messrs. Brown and Smith feel small.

Her contribution in the meeting was a Crossed Transaction — that is, instead of responding from the Nurturing Parent ego state that was asked for, she chose to reply from the Critical Parent, and to change the whole feeling of the meeting.

There was every likelihood that after that somebody else would have jumped up to say something scathing to make her look small in turn. A verbal fight is often the outcome of such a crossed transaction. However, Mrs. Black was one of those apparently natural peacemakers who poured oil on the troubled waters of that meeting.

Mrs. Black's contribution was also a Crossed Transaction. (Diag. 8) Instead of accepting Mrs. Blue's invitation to go into put-down Child, she went into her Adult and looked at the actual facts of the situation under discussion. She avoided spending more time on the hurts and the prejudices under the surface of the discussion, which might not have been appropriate items for airing at a business meeting.

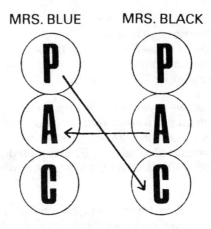

MRS. BLUE   MRS. BLACK

8.   *A Crossed Transaction—but a positive confrontation.*

If you want to change the feeling-level of a conversation, then use a different ego state from the one expected by the previous remark. But choose carefully which ego state to use, because Crossed transactions can give a lot of hurt, or they can be for healing through confrontation.

It is very important for the health of the church that Christians learn to confront each other lovingly. Confrontation which springs from anger is usually unlovingly handled and often aims to diminish the other person rather than to be for his growth.

Christians can be people to whom others turn for help and guidance. The alternative to fostering a string of dependent relationships is often to develop the ability to confront by crossing transactions. If you are a person to whom others turn, what do you do or say when someone says to you, yet again, "Please tell me what I should do. I don't seem to be able to think straight. You always seem to know the right thing to do."

That person expects you to talk with her in a series of complementary transactions, with her playing the "helpless Child" and you accepting the role of "all-wise Parent". If you do, she will come back again and again. You will be in great demand, but she will not grow up. It can almost seem to her like a betrayal the first time you have the courage to cross the transaction, and from your Adult, invite her to use her Adult with a phrase like, "What are your options in this situation?" It's worth persevering if you truly want her to be able to make decisions for herself.

The last type of transaction is called an "Ulterior Transaction". This can either be good fun and be a sign of closeness and fellowship or it can be the opposite — an indication that someone is feeling very insecure and on the defensive, ready to hit below the belt.

The word "ulterior" indicates that something is going on below the surface of what appears to be a straightforward communication. An apparently innocent remark like, "Of course, the Sunday School is Stan's whole life!" could either convey to the hearer the information that in Stan the church has a most devoted superintendent of Sunday School, or else it could have been said in sarcasm and imply, "And there's no use expecting Stan to support any **other** aspect of the church's life." Normally with an ulterior transaction there is a tone of voice or facial expression that conveys the "under the surface" meaning clearly to anyone who will pick it up.

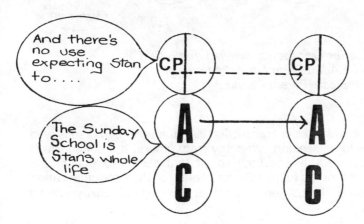

9. *The beginning of an Ulterior Transaction.*

Teasing can be another form of ulterior transaction when the victim is caught between replying to what has been actually said, or responding to what has been implied by the non-verbal communication.

31

Sometimes, even in church committees, a series of apparently innocent questions can be used with deadly effect to lead a person into a verbal corner where he can be pounced upon with a self-righteous ''Now I've got you!'' final statement, revealing the ulterior nature of the questioning, and leaving the person questioned feeling exposed and trapped. Is this ''speaking the truth in love''? (Diag. 10)

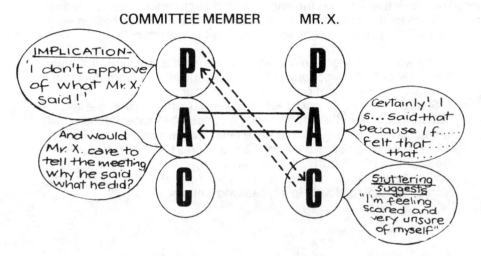

10. *An Ulterior Transaction where what is said could be Adult - Adult, but the tones of voice indicate Parent - Child.*

Another form of ulterior transaction is indulged in by persons who seem always to be seeking sympathy from others. It's not so much what they say as the way they say it that seems to manipulate others into responding to the ulterior content of their communication and into doing things for them that they could easily do for themselves.

And what about the positive forms of ulterior transactions? These normally spring from good experiences shared with others. Imagine a church family camp which has reached its final evening. One of the leaders can make a speech which to any outsider might seem either boring or without much significance but the entire company who has shared the week's experiences together can be rocking with laughter. (Diag. 11)

Certain words have become ''in'' langauge during the week for the campers.

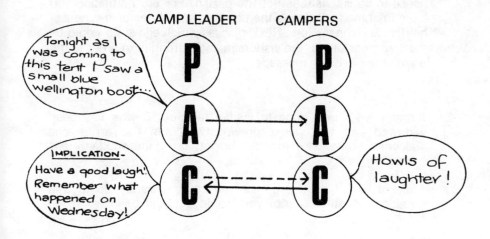

11. A 'good fun' Ulterior Transaction where the audience responds to the underlying implication, not to the words actually said.

They all pick up the ulterior significance of the innocent words being spoken and it deepens the feeling of togetherness in the group. (Of course, it can invite an outsider to feel very much out in the cold if people are inconsiderate enough not to put him in the picture if the campers go on using ''in'' language in his company after camp is over.)

Whether they be between two people or many more, loving relationships thrive best on fresh new experiences of togetherness as well as with a significant shared history. An ulterior transaction based on the church family camp of last week still has significance, but it can become threadbare nine months later! Maintaining the fun in communicating with ulterior transactions needs a steady fresh supply of shared meaningful happenings. Make time for them!

For you to think through by yourself, or with others.

1. In small groups, imagine typical short excerpts of conversation
   you might encounter if you went from the local church on a
   house-to-house visitation of the parish. For each situation you
   have imagined, diagnose the possible ego states of the house-
   holders and the visitors. Next, discuss which ego state would be
   most appropriate for the visitors in each situation in order to get
   across the Christian message.

2. Imagine you have gone to visit a lady of 50 who has been
   widowed just two weeks previously. When you arrive she
   welcomes you and seems very bright, but quite suddenly she
   bursts into tears.

   Make a list of all the things you could possibly do in that
   situation (whether or not you would actually be likely to do
   them).

   When your list is complete, go down each item, checking off
   whether that would be a P, A, or C reaction on your part.

   Which ego state would the lady be in? Which ego state might
   she need to feel from you?

   Discuss your answers in small groups.

3. A person has begun to come to you quite regularly for advice.
   Each time, she hooks into your Parent to meet the needs of her
   Child. You are now feeling she is becoming far too dependent
   on you. Write out a conversation in which you successfully cross
   a transaction so that she begins to think for herself.

4. In pairs, role-play a married couple or a pair of close friends
   having a crossed transaction argument where feelings are
   getting hurt. When you've had enough, let one of the couple
   try to cross the transaction helpfully to begin to deal with the
   hurt feelings instead of the subject of the argument.

34

MINI-CASE STUDIES

Here are 3 short case studies. Select one that interests you.

Instructions: In a small group, discuss how the people involved in the transaction might be feeling, then diagnose from which ego state/s the stimulus is being sent, and from which ego state/s the response is being sought.

After that, think up three possible responses — one from each ego state, and finally, come to some conclusion as to which would be the most appropriate response for building up a healthy on-going relationship.

SITUATION A: Mr. Brown is a man actively involved in community concerns and well-known in his neighbourhood for this. One evening a woman in her late thirties arrived at his door asking to talk with him. Taking her into his home, he invited her to sit down and then asked what he could do for her.

Looking as if she might burst into tears at any moment, she replied, "It's my son. I can't do a thing with him. You have to help me. Everyone knows that you can handle things, so I want you to tell me what to do."

SITUATION B: Mrs. McLeod is a widow in her early fifties. Since the death of her husband and the marriage of her two children she has become involved in the local church's Caring Action Group. At work at the tea break one morning she was chatting to a colleague about a fund-raising effort the group was organising to hire a mini-bus for a summer outing for some senior citizens. Quite unexpectedly, the colleague cut in with, "That's what's wrong with you Christians, of course. Why are you always interfering? Why don't you let the families of the old folk look after their own? You should learn to mind your own business!"

SITUATION C: Jim is a leader in the local Christian cafe. The set-up attracts many youngsters with no church connection, and many with unsettled home backgrounds. Delia is fourteen and has very recently begun to come around the cafe, having joined up with some of the quieter girls to become a rather precocious ring-leader for them. As Jim passes the table at which this group is sitting one evening Delia puts her arm around him and makes a very suggestive remark.

CHAPTER 5.

WHAT DO YOU DO WITH YOUR FEELINGS?

Trading stamps.

* Do you ever bottle up your feelings until you give yourself a headache?

* Have you ever heard someone saying, "Well, that's the last straw! I'm never going to talk to him again"?

* How do you celebrate when a series of good experiences comes your way and you feel really great?

Nowadays people have grown familiar with the idea of trading stamps being given at the purchase of certain goods. Many folk collect them, save them up and cash them in when they have enough to exchange for something they want. Transactional Analysis uses this as a analogy for what people do with their feelings.

Feelings come in the course of everyday living, and are experienced as positive or negative. Often people learning Transactional Analysis become increasingly aware of their feelings as they experience the Child ego state within them as a reality.

A small child often exhibits raw feelings of anger, fear, frustration bewilderment, love, happiness, contentment, curiosity, temper, unhappiness and so on in a way that grown-up people rarely give themselves permission to express. But even the most controlled, grown-up, apparently unfeeling person collects feelings, saves them up, and cashes them in, in his Child ego state.

In early childhood, even before a child starts collecting beetles and postage stamps, match-boxes and Dinky toys, he will have begun a pattern of collecting feelings, saving them up and cashing them in. A little child begins collecting particular feelings in order to survive or to enhance his survival in a world where power belongs to big people. There are other feelings he will seem to have no interest in saving up, although he may well receive them. Using his intuition the child will soon figure out what feelings he should collect, and what feelings are not rewarded in his small life-world. His parents might continually threaten him with "Just wait till your father comes home!" or "You're going to land up in the home for bad girls and boys!", and so he soon knows how it feels to save up 'fear' stamps. If he constantly hears "You stupid boy! Why didn't you do what I told you?", he will get the message that 'stupid' stamps are for him to collect. If his mother never gets 'angry' but only 'deeply hurt' by his naughtiness, he may well pick up that 'anger' stamps mustn't even be received by his family, but that saving up 'hurt' stamps is a highly respectable pursuit.

Fortunately, people also save up positive feelings, and very soon are able so to arrange life for themselves that they ensure an adequate supply of good stamps to cash at will. A little three-year-old can have already worked out for herself a scheme for receiving positive attention from grown-ups which includes an endless supply of cuddles and kisses and pats on the head for her, and plenty of good feelings for the grown-ups who respond so positively to her.

In Transactional Analysis, stamps are often referred to by certain colours which seem to indicate certain feelings for most people. For instance, collecting positive feelings is sometimes called collecting GOLD STAMPS; GREEN STAMPS are for jealousy, BROWN or GREY for depression, WHITE for selfrighteousness, RED for anger, and so on.

So, through life, incidents take place, transactions occur, and the folk involved receive positive or negative feelings as a result. Everybody has some stamps they don't need to save up. Perhaps they never have saved up one particular kind of feeling — for example, some person may never have needed to save up green stamps for jealousy. In certain situations she might feel "That looks good. I wouldn't mind having one of those for myself", but there the feeling stops — the stamp has been crumpled up and put in the bin because that person has no need to save up jealousy stamps and cash them in. Another person might have a real need to save up red stamps for anger. He will go through life allowing himself to get angry and frustrated by one situation after another, all the while saving up the red stamps until he feels justified in cashing them in. How he will cash them in depends on what he finds acceptable behaviour in himself at the time.

He might cash them in by getting a tension headache, by driving over the speed limit, by having a fight with his wife over some apparently trivial matter, by taking on far more work than he can reasonably cope with, by going out and getting drunk, by being late for an important meeting . . . he may even save up enough books of red stamps to justify for himself the possibility of committing murder, or suing for a divorce.

When a person 'cashes in' negative feelings, he does so in behaviour which is inappropriate to the here-and-now situation, and so cashing in of negative stamps leads on to the collection and saving up of more negative feelings.

Saving up and cashing in negative feelings is damaging to relation -ships; saving up and cashing in gold stamps can be a lot more enjoyable. One of the paradoxes in being typically Scottish is that, although we have the (quite undeserved) reputation of being tight-fisted with our gold, we are often pig-headed enough not even to pick up a gold stamp that is handed to us! Someone says something really complimentary to us and, instead of collecting a good feeling, we think, ''What's she wanting?'' Authentically sharing good feelings with others will often result in us collecting gold stamps in return. Giving good feelings to folk sets them free to give good feelings to others!

Each person has his own pattern of which feelings he collects, which he saves up, and of how he cashes them in. Since the pattern begins in early childhood, it is familiar and feels 'safe' to the grown-up who perpetuates it. He knows how to handle these feelings, and the people he relates to often accept his methods of 'cashing-in' as part of his nature unless the pattern is very destructuve towards himself or others.

But basic to Christianity is the belief that human nature can change. Many Christians have experienced dramatic changes in their feelings taking place under the influence of the Holy Spirit, but there always does seem a place for steady, disciplined work on ourselves where we accept the responsibility for our feelings and subsequent actions, and with his help and forgiveness strive towards the love we know to be our heritage.

In this work, many have found Transactional Analysis to be a tool of practical use, especially when wielded within a loving and supportive Christian community.

Once a person identifies her particular pattern of cashing in negative feelings inappropriately, she can begin to work on changing it. She can enlist the help of others in confronting her when they are at the receiving end of the cashing-in, and together they can trace back through the saving up process using a helpful combination of their Adult ego state and their Nurturing Parent resources that care for the Child within, to discover and create ways of dealing with the negative feelings in an appropriate manner as and when they arise. It takes practice and patience, but new ways of loving can come from such sharing.

For you to think through by yourself, or with others.

1. Think of a pattern of behaviour you have in which you make other people miserable because of how you are feeling.

    Think up a way of dealing more creatively and positively with your feelings so you can look after them when you collect them, and have no need to save them up and punish yourself and others by cashing them in.

2. Which kinds of trading stamps do you think were saved up by the following Biblical characters and how did they cash them in?

    a) Martha of Bethany (Luke 10: 38 - 42)

    b) Jonah (Jonah 4)

    c) Queen Jezebel and King Ahab (1 Kings 21)

3. Imagine the following situation. Somebody on a church committee begins to criticise the way things are being run and tells how much better things were in his previous church. Discuss in small groups:

    a) What kind of feelings are likely to be being collected by other committee members?

    b) How might they cash them in?

    c) What body language might make you aware that bad feelings were being collected by the committee?

    d) What action could be taken by somebody to deal with the feelings without having to cash them in?

e) What further positive action might be taken by the group to help the original speaker not to cash in his trading stamps again in such a critical manner?

4. Many people save up feelings and cash them in on their own bodies by developing slight — or more serious — psychosomatic symptoms.

If something is not going well for you, which muscles do you tense up? Which of your body's organs become upset? Share this in pairs.

Next, tell each other how you normally cope with this tension.

Then discuss what you plan to do the next time you feel this happening. Make sure that what you decide to do deals with the feelings you collect as well as their bodily symptoms.

CHAPTER 6

I'M O.K. YOU'RE O.K.

Life positions

* Do you know anyone who is constantly underselling herself and is quite convinced that everyone else is far more capable than she?

* Do you know anyone who keeps putting other people down and will rarely take the blame for anything he does or says?

* Have you ever been with someone who seemed to believe in you in a way that helped you to be a better person and at the same time seemed to respect and accept his own value as a human being?

From birth — and even, some say, before that — our experience of being a person among other persons leads us to adopt attitudes towards ourselves and others.

Much has recently been written about the frightening experience birth itself can be to a virtually helpless morsel of humanity. Certainly, even with the most loving and attentive parents, each infant must experience times of fear and anxiety just because he has no way of understanding what is happening to him in this world of powerful giants.

A baby can waken in a dark room alone and his crying might not awaken his parents. A toddler who has happily occupied the centre of attention of two doting parents might, for no apparent reason, discover that her mother is becoming tired, clumsy and less patient with her and then out of the blue disappears for five bewildering days, only to return with a baby boy who seems far more important to her parents than she now is. A little three year old can get lost in a maze of grown-ups' legs in a crowded supermarket and find himself surrounded by complete strangers who want to pick him up and carry him away to somewhere strange called 'the Manager's Office'.

And when a child is not wanted, loved and cared for, the conclusions he can arrive at about himself and others, can be quite justified.

Very early in life a little person comes to a conclusion about himself and others emotionally significant to him on the basis of his response to experiences of life which he is not equipped fully to understand. This conclusion is adopted as an attitude and, time and again, throughout his life, when things go wrong for him, he will almost automatically slip back into this attitude to himself and others because it is the one that seemed to help him survive through the early years.

There are three basic negative LIFE POSITIONS expressed in Transactional Analysis terminology as:—

I'M NOT O.K.   —   YOU'RE O.K.
I'M O.K.   —   YOU'RE NOT O.K.
I'M NOT O.K.   —   YOU'RE NOT O.K.

The phrase "O.K." is taken straight from childhood experience. It is not a rationally definable term. It is rather the expression of an attitude full of Child feelings about himself and others in his world. It expresses the child's response to whether he feels accepted and loved and whether he can accept and love others. "O.K." is not to be understood in theological or moral terms.

Experience indicates that a person's basic life position is negative. Often he is not aware that he has adopted it, although his behaviour under stress demonstrates it. From time to time, each person will experience himself in any one of the life positions. If the one he is in is not his basic negative one, then it is for him a "GOING LIFE POSITION" for that situation.

It is often easier to spot the basic life position of some other person than it is to discover one's own. People who come across as being frequently in their Critical Parent and as justifying their own actions are in the "I'm O.K. — You're not O.K." category. Those who are often belittling themselves and their abilities, but admiring other people and depending on them are usually in the position "I'm not O.K. — You're O.K." while the double negative of "I'm not O.K. — You're not O.K." shows up in those who bear a grudge against life and think of themselves as losers. No basic negative life position is any better or more to be blamed than any other. They were all formed long before each little person could make rational decisions, and they all contribute towards bad relationships with other people.

This appears to be rather a depressing way to begin forming relationships, but of course it is only part of the truth about our attitudes. By far the majority of people have good, close, loving, accepting relationships and experiences in childhood alongside the ones that scare them. Over and over again they have experiences from the only positive life position — "I'm O.K. — You're O.K." — when things are going well for all concerned.

The reason why Transactional Analysis points out the influence of the basic negative life position is that it was adopted in the age of fantasy when bad experiences seemed like struggles for survival. When an adult takes refuge from an unpleasant happening or relationship by reverting to her basic negative life position, she ceases to relate to the reality of the here and now. Instead, she relates inappropriately by underestimating or by over-estimating her own and other people's strengths and weaknesses.

Jesus is for us the supreme illustration of someone who related to others in the "I'm O.K. — You're O.K." position. His attitude recorded in the Gospel stories to people he encountered set them free to become the people he believed they could become.

His handling of the incident when the Pharisees brought to him the woman caught in the act of adultery illustrates this beautifully. He believed in the moral self-awareness of the Pharisees enough to say to them, "Whichever one of you has committed no sin may throw the first stone at her." — and nobody did. And he believed enough in the woman's desire to be different to say to her, "I do not condemn you either. Go, but do not sin again." John 8:11.

In our experience of teaching T.A. in the church, it is this phrase "I'm O.K. You're O.K." that seems to give Christians most trouble. We have often encountered bewildered looks accompanied by questions like, "But what about original sin?" or, "But how can I be 'O.K.' since I am basically a sinner in the eyes of God?"

T.A. is not a theology. It therefore does not have a doctrine of God nor a doctrine of sin. T.A. is a theory about human relationships. If a person who chooses to use T.A. also is a Christian and believes in God and in sin, does this give him a different attitude to his fellow beings than the non-Christian who uses T.A.? What is the Christian's attitude to himself and others? Does a Christian believe that because his neighbour is a sinner he must treat him like dirt? Does a Christian believe that because he himself is a sinner, he must

44

despise and ill-treat himself? Unfortunately there are a few Christians who have this attitude to themselves and others and they are usually unhappy, unkind and unfriendly people.

Most Christians, however, believe something different — something we might write like this. "I am a sinner, but Jesus Christ died to set me free from my sin to be one of God's children. To him I am infinitely precious. Because I am loved by him, I can love myself and others. I can relate to them as if they too are of infinite value . . . because I believe they are.

Beside that, the phrase "O.K." somehow fades into near insignificance!

Strangely enough, although T.A. has nothing to say about sin (that being a theological term) what the theory does say, is that although it is possible for people to have the attitudes to themselves and others of "I'm O.K. You're O.K.", mostly, they don't. And that is when relationships begin to go wrong. In fact, T.A. goes even further and says that persons do not basically have a positive attitude to themselves and others; that what it calls the Basic Life Positions are, in fact, negative. The one truly positive one (I'm O.K. You're O.K.) is the one to be worked for if you want to relate well to others. And that to me sounds very like what Paul said in 1 Cor. 14:1!

To be aware of the theory of Life Positions is good for Christians. To change from the negatives to the positive is something to be doggedly worked at, but we believe we are not left alone in the struggle. We have Christ's forgiveness when we slip back, and his strength to go forward. We also have around us the support and encouragement of the Christian community, so we ought increasingly to be, with all that, in the free "I'm O.K. You're O.K." position. We have resources for change far beyond the limitations we normally impose upon ourselves!

For you to think through by yourself, or with others

1.   Which do you think is your Basic Negative Life Position?

To discover this, go back to last week, to last year, to five, ten, twenty years ago. . . and pick out incidents you remember because they were bad for you, or for others involved with you. For each one ask yourself, 'in this situation am I feeling 'O.K.' or 'not O.K.' about myself? . . . and am I feeling 'You're O.K.' or 'You're not O.K.' about the others involved? You will find a pattern which shows your attitude to yourself and others.

45

2. In a small group, take the four Life Positions and discuss how a person operating from each of these would be likely to handle the following situations:

a) being criticised

b) being praised

c) being in competition

d) working in a partnership

e) being the chairperson of a committee.

3. From your memory of their behaviour, guess which Life Position was the most common one for each of the following Biblical characters:

a) Ruth

b) Joseph

c) Saul of Tarsus

d) Moses

e) Mary Magdalene

f) King Saul.

4. Which of the four Life Positions do you think your local congregation holds as regards itself and non-members in the community?

CHAPTER 7

THE GAMES PEOPLE PLAY

Psychological games

*   Do you ever have the uncomfortable feeling that someone is pretending to be interested in you, but is only waiting for the chance to put you down?

*   Have you seen someone leading another person on sexually by a mild flirtation and then claiming injured innocence when the other rises to the bait?

*   Are you aware that some people kid themselves that they can cope with accepting so many commitments that they have a breakdown?

What is going on when these situations happen?

In everyday life when it is said that people are 'playing games' with each other, this can mean anything from underhand manipulation to harmless good fun. In Transactional Analysis, the term "GAME" means PSYCHOLOGICAL GAME — and that is never good fun. Eric Berne has devoted a whole book to them in his best-seller "Games People Play".[1] He gives the games colloquial names which help in their quick identification.

A psychological game is a series of manipulations between people which has the effect of being dramatic, but of spoiling the relationship. It is in fact a series of ulterior transactions.

People involved in a psychological game can end up feeling hurt, rejected, depressed, jealous, self-righteous, or any number of negative feelings.

On the surface, all appears 'above board', but something unhappy is going on underneath. People operate on the surface or social level, and also behave towards each other beneath the surface at the psychological level. Psychological games are basically dishonest.

47

People only play psychological games when they slip out of the "I'm O.K. You're O.K." attitude into one of the negative life positions. It's almost as if we need reconvincing that we — or others — are "not O.K.".

Any procedure which is heavily stroke-oriented is enticing for the average human being, and if positive strokes are either not forthcoming or are too threatening for the people involved, then there is an attraction towards a psychological games-playing way of relating, because in games we give and receive negative strokes.

Like all other ways of relating, games are first observed and then copied in early childhood. The little child makes up his mind which attitude he will adopt towards himself and others, and when bad experiences come (when he will go into his basic negative life position) he will choose to relate through psychological games which reinforce this attitude over and over again as others join in his games.

For instance, a little girl might have had experiences from which she concluded "I'm O.K. You're not O.K.". She would then set out unconsciously to reinforce this, and might do so by choosing the common childhood game of "Mine is better than yours". The scene is set if she has a younger brother to manipulate.

A game might take place one day when she was bored and needed something exciting to do, or the young brother might be needing some attention and so have come to interrupt whatever she was engrossed in thus giving her an excuse to be annoyed. How could she cash in in these situations?

Perhaps she could cheat him at a game of Snakes and Ladders, or she could prove that she could run faster or climb higher or make paper aeroplanes which flew further. She would appear to be playing away contentedly with him should their mother arrive on the scene, but she would actually be getting even with life by waiting till the young brother was enjoying her attention and then delivering him a nasty negative stroke with a "Mine is better than yours" trick. His reaction to being victimised would then reinforce her "I'm O.K. You're not O.K." position.

If this situation were to be repeated often enough (with subtle differences) then the little brother might well decide "I'm not O.K. You're O.K." (she always wins so she must be "O.K.") and begin to initiate the games-playing by deliberately annoying her, and so inviting her to play "Kick me" with him. This would reinforce his life position which would call for receiving negative strokes from others.

When these children grow up it is likely they will choose life partners who will fit in by playing perhaps more sophisticated versions of these games, and thus keep them in old familiar patterns of relationship from which they once sought the negative strokes they needed in order to survive. Married couples often have complementary basic· negative life positions, and when their relationship is under tension for any reason, will start up psychological games that fit into each other's familiar patterns and hinder their growth in love and understanding.

A psychological game enables people to avoid the threat of vulnerability that they fear in getting close to others while at the same time gets them needed attention even though that consists of negative strokes.

If you want to spot a psychological game in action, then look out for people playing any of three special roles — the roles of Persecutor, Rescuer or Victim. They are often diagrammed thus, because players tend to switch from one role to another as a game proceeds.

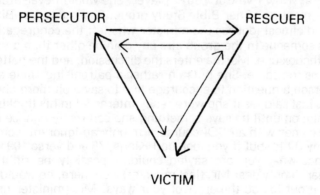

PERSECUTOR   RESCUER

VICTIM

A Persecutor criticises or otherwise puts down others who don't need or deserve it. A Rescuer rushes in to help those who would be better to help themselves and a Victim behaves as if he deserves persecuting or needs rescuing — but in actual fact deserves or needs neither. These are roles which are learned in childhood.

A few examples might illustrate this. Imagine a "Harried" player. His name is Phil. He is very popular and capable, and is one of those people who finds it difficult to say no if asked to do something. In fact, if he's in a situation where it seems as if no-one else is about to volunteer for a job, Phil will volunteer himself. When people think over who they can ask to do something Phil's name comes popping into their minds. He is always so willing. Phil finds it very difficult to delegate work to others. Phil is a born Rescuer. He takes on things that others could easily do who haven't his special abilities. People around Phil often do not get the chance to shoulder responsibility or to try out new tasks — thus in a very subtle way, Phil is victimising them. Then comes the day when Phil has taken on too much. He feels really under pressure. He feels like a Victim for all the others who have asked him to do things. Instead of sorting out his tasks realistically and delegating work to others so that he can manage, Phil allows things to get into such a mess that several people become Victim, then switch to Persecutor as they allow Phil to feel their exasperation with him. Poor Phil . . . . he began as Rescuer and ended up Victim. Others acted as Victim for him, then switched to Persecutor. Phil's basic life position which he goes back to in times of crisis is "I'm not O.K. You're not O.K." (I'm not O.K., so I have to do things for people so they will accept me. You're not O.K. because you don't have all the abilities I have)

Martha is a "Now I've Got You!" player. She would never dream of missing a meeting of her Bible Study group. She knows her Bible very well and almost idolises the minister who left the congregation last year. If someone in the group airs any opinion other than a very safe and orthodox one, Martha enters the discussion, and the pattern always seems the same. She puts on rather a patronising smile and asks the person a question to encourage him to say a bit more about what he has just said, as if she were really interested in his thinking. She leads him on until he says something she can really pounce on, then in she comes with an "Of course, I'm only an ignorant woman who loves my Bible, but if you look up I Kings, 73 and verse 109 you will find that what you are saying couldn't possibly be right!". Or, "Oh dear, if only dear Mr. (last minister) were here, he would be able to point out to you the error of your ways. Mr. (minister now) hasn't yet got his years of experience to help you, of course." Martha at first appears to be Rescuing. From there she switches to being Victim ('only an ignorant woman') then comes right in on her Victim in a triumphant Persecutor role. From feeling encouraged and helped to think things through, the young man who ventured the new idea has ended up psychologically bound, gagged and condemned — thoroughly Victim.

A Games Grid of some Psychological Games

THEME	NAME OF THE GAME	PURPOSE TO PROVE	MAIN ROLE
Blaming Others	'If it weren't for you 'See what you made me do' Rapo Blemish	You're not O.K.	Perscutor
Saving Others	'I'm only trying to help you' 'What would you do without me' Harried	You're not O.K.	Rescuer
Provoking Put-Downs	'Kick me' 'Stupid' Wooden Leg 'Yes. . . but'	I'm not O.K. You're not O.K. or I'm not O.K.	Victim Persecutor or Victim
Getting Even	'Now I've got you' 'Mine is better yours'	You're not O.K.	Persecutor

Descriptions of some Games

"KICK ME" is seen in behaviour which encourages or invites others to give a put-down, or a negative stroke to the person initiating the game. It is very similar to two other games — "Poor Me", and "Stupid".

"NOW I'VE GOT YOU!" demonstrates behaviour which manipulates the other person into the position of appearing to be in the wrong.

"YES — BUT" is a succession of refusals of offers of help which have been invited by the player initiating the game, in order to prove that other people are useless or that the person initiating the game is helpless.

51

HARRIED is a game in which a person says 'yes' to everything until his time is overflowing with unfinished business. This has an increasingly negative effect upon his personality and relationships until his health fails, or he has a breakdown. In doing this he exaggerates his own strength and other people's weakness.

RAPO is a sexual game initiated by a person of either sex flirting with a member of the opposite sex, and giving out messages to imply willingness to develop the relationship. When he or she responds to the ulterior psychological level of the transaction, the initiator turns Persecutor and claims that the Victim is making improper advances to him/her and has completely misunderstood her/his innocent offer of friendship.

BLEMISH In this game, what seems like praise gets spoiled by some qualifying remark. "You're all right . . . except for . . ."

WOODEN LEG The initiator claims some disability in order to evade personal responsibility. 'What can you expect from me, I've got a wooden leg (a handicap, I'm the wrong age, sex, I've got the wrong background, etc.)'.

"IF IT WEREN'T FOR YOU" is played by persons who don't take responsibility for their share in making relationships work, or putting other plans into action. They store up petty resentments against the others involved with them, then lay all the blame at their feet when the chips are down.

How to stop games

1. One's own games

   A person can practice becoming aware of the particular games he is accustomed to initiate. He can recognise the specific feelings to which he repeatedly returns. His basic life-position can be identified. He can stop playing Rescuer — helping those who don't need help, or playing Persecutor, criticising those who don't deserve it, or playing Victim, acting helpless or dependent when really able to stand on his own feet. To prevent a game he can stop exaggerating his own strengths and weaknesses. Choosing to give and accept positive strokes is an effective way of refusing to engage in games-playing.

2. Other people's games

   A method of stopping someone else's game is to refuse to play the corresponding hand in the game. A person can stop exaggerating the strengths and weaknesses of the other. He can refuse to accept negative strokes and he can give positive strokes. If this happens, the conditions in which a game can exist are withdrawn.

(A sure way NOT to stop someone else's game is to point out to him that he is playing a game in such a way that this move is a "Now I've got you!" in itself).

Pick up any book which tells of the way people relate to each other and psychological games will be recorded. The Bible is an account of the lives or ordinary sinful men and women like ourselves, so it is no exception. The difference is seen in the Gospels where it is recorded time and again how individuals or groups tried to inveigle Jesus into playing their psychological games. Invariably he stopped their games by refusing to relate to them in this negative way. One such story is that of the man with the crippled hand. (Luke 6). The Pharisees deliberately placed him in the congregation where Jesus was to teach to trap him into healing him on the Sabbath. They were planning for a game of "Now I've got you!". Jesus refused to become their Victim and to allow them to become his Persecutors. He confronted them with their ability to see that compassion was more important to God than legalism, and so he stopped their game.

When a person is in the "I'm O.K. — You're O.K." position, he has no need to play psychological games.

1. *Games People Play, Eric Berne.*

For you to think through by yourself, or with others

1. From the descriptions given of psychological games, which ones have you spotted that you play?

   Which have you spotted that are played in your church?

   How can you go about stopping playing your part in these?

2. Look at some of the Psychological Games played in the Bible.

   Identify   a) Who is playing which Game Role?
                 b) Which Basic Negative Life Position is being reinforced for the initiator?
                 c) What feeling do the characters end with?

Passages: Genesis 25:29-34; 27:33-36 (Jacob and Esau)
Genesis 37 (Joseph)
Luke 19:20-24 (Parable of the Talents)
Judges 16 (Samson)

3. In the following passages, people try to play Games but are stopped. Identify the Game Role of the initiator and his Basic Negative Life Position and the Game he is trying to play; but then spot who steps in to stop the Game from the position "I'm O.K.: You're O.K.".

Passages: Luke 6:6-11   The Man with the Paralysed Hand
John 5:1-9   The Healing at the Pool of Bethesda
John 8:2-11   The Woman Caught in Adultery
Exodus 18   Jethro's Visit to Moses
1 Kings 19:1-18 Elijah on Mount Horeb

4. Which Games have been passed on in your family from the previous generation to you? How are you going to help your children (if you have any) to stop playing these same Games?

CHAPTER 8

HOW DO YOU USE TIME?

Time Structuring

★ What do you do when you are standing in a bus queue?

★ How do you most enjoy spending time in a group with others?

★ Do you use time today in the way your family taught you?

As people, we seem to have a need to structure the time we have with other people. Eric Berne called this 'structure hunger'. Those who founded enclosed religious orders often devised a structure for each day to govern how members of the order should relate to each other, and when. People who are made redundant from work, or who are recently retired often find the lack of superimposed structure for their day very hard to cope with, and set about providing some structure for themselves.

When Berne wrote about this, he itemised six different ways of structuring time with others, and listed them in order of stroke intensity. Here is his list:
Withdrawal
Ritual
Pastimes
Activities
Games
Intimacy

These ways can be seen in the relationship of two people as easily as they can in what happens when a group gets together. To illustrate Time Structuring, let's think of Sue and Jack, and the house group that meets in their home.

1. Withdrawal

Sue and Jack are a young married couple. They enjoy hillwalking together. For long stretches of time they will be walking along without talking, each thinking their own thoughts. Often that will be in companionable silence: occasionally they will have quarrelled, and withdrawn from each other to 'lick their wounds'. Withdrawal, in T.A. terms, is a way of structuring time during which the only strokes you are actually receiving are those you are giving yourself. You are drawing on your bank of strokes remembered. After a quarrel, Jack may withdraw to go over and over hurtful things Sue has said after he disagreed with her: Sue may be remembering a recent discussion on a similar topic with her close friend Mary, where Mary had agreed with her opinion, and had appreciated what she had said.

At the meeting of their house group there are two members who rarely contribute much to discussions, but who, when asked, will say something about what they have been thinking while others have talked. "Everyone else seems to put things so much better than I can. I'm quite content to sit and listen", or, "By the time I get around to thinking how to say something, someone else has already said it." During Withdrawal, these members are probably having internal dialogue between their Child and Critical Parent ego states reminiscent of the actual conversations their parents had with them when they were children.

People can engage in withdrawal in any ego state. Sue is one of the house group leaders, and often while people are talking she is silently active in her Adult, thinking through what is happening in the group, and figuring out when to break in to move on to the next topic. In Nurturing Parent, Jack might be aware that the subject under discussion has brought a tear to the eye of a member recently widowed, and be deciding how he might look after her.

2. Ritual

A ritual is an acceptable and repetitive pattern of behaviour for those engaged in it. Sometimes it begins at a time of great significance in the lives of those involved, and then it is perpetuated by them, bringing with it its own emotional security. At other times a Ritual is just what the couple always does, done in the way they always do it. The way they set the dinner table: the order in which they use the bathroom in the mornings. The tone of voice in which they say "And how was your day, dear?" Each person involved in Ritual knows what will happen next. A Ritual is a series of predetermined transactions.

Early in their marriage, Sue and Jack had a quarrel when hill-walking. They both went into Withdrawal. Eventually both wanted to begin talking again, but felt afraid that the talk might lead to more quarrelling. On they walked in silence, till Sue could bear it no longer. She slipped her hand into Jack's. Jack held her hand tightly for a few paces, and then his fingers twirled her wedding ring. Afterwards, when they put the experience into words, he said that his action meant remembering the phrase in their wedding service "for better or for worse." Since then, that non-verbal transaction has become a Ritual for them to use when they are prepared to stop a quarrel. The house group members have slipped into Ritual with the structured programme they have set for each time they meet. Sue or Jack always answers the door bell's ring with a "Hi there! Good to see you." And the response they normally receive is "Good to be here again!" - a twostroke Ritual. Once everyone has arrived, the person leading the group will begin by explaining the reason for the absence of any missing member, and then will say, "Well, let's begin with a prayer." In the prayer, the leader always prays for the missing group members. At the cup of tea time, the leader always begins by passing round a biscuit from which each member takes a tiny bit, eats it, then passes it on to the next member, who repeats the process in silence. This Ritual came from a discussion on the Last Supper, and has significance for this group. Before the group disperses each night, they link hands with each other and say together "The grace of the Lord Jesus Christ be with us all." When new members join the house group, the ritual of the passing of the biscuit is explained to them in detail. At the end, the leader usually says "We hold hands to bless each other before we go," but no-one thinks to explain the other Rituals. Group members pick them up as they gradually feel they belong, and begin to feel stroked by them. Most relationships contain Ritual without the people concerned consciously realising it is an accepted and repetitive way they have of structuring their time together.

3. **Pastimes**

Pastimes are ways in which we converse with other people with no particular agenda except to pass the time pleasantly. Sometimes Sue and Jack will switch on television without caring much which programme they view. As they watch, their conversation will be Pastiming: "Doesn't that man remind you of old Mr. Brown round the corner?" "This is very pleasant. The scenery is beautiful." "Can't stand her voice! Glad you don't sound like that, dear." It's the kind of conversation they have had together in the past, and it feels comfortably familiar to them, although the content will have changed slightly from the last time. They often Pastime as they picnic in the hills. "Isn't it a lovely day?" "Do you remember the time we saw a stag with massive antlers on that crag over there?"

Pastiming conversation is not geared to end in any action, and generally it is a series of complementary transactions. People get the responses they expect from other people.

Just as Eric Berne named Games, so he sometimes gave names to Pastiming, highlighting the themes of Pastiming conversations. Occasionally the house group will slip into Pastiming named "Isn't it awful?", where all the group members make remarks from Critical Parent ego states about something currently in the news. Often the kind of conversations that happen as the group gathers is Pastiming - "The weather", or "Saturday's game", "Films I have seen", or "Fundraising as I have known it." To avoid controversy, Pastiming has a large Adapted Child component. For the sake of peace, people agree with one another, avoiding crossed transactions.

The difference between Games and Pastiming is that in Pastimes, there are no role switches nor ulterior transactions.

4. Activities

When Sue and Jack are having a picnic on one of their hill-climbing expeditions, they sometimes switch from Pastiming to Activity in their conversation. "Which route should we take home from here?" "Let's go the shorter one - I'm beginning to feel a blister on my heel."

Activity is task-oriented, designed to achieve a goal. When people are relating in this way they have a purpose to their conversation. Often Activity is Adult ego state level conversation.

In the house group, Jack once said, "There seems to be some confusion amongst us as to what the word 'love' really means. Let's try to make up a definition for it, so we all know what we mean when we use the word." The discussion following that, was Activity.

Sue and Jack videoed a programme on homelessness and used it at the housegroup to spark off a discussion on what the housegroup might do about it in their city. Sue and Jack watched the programme beforehand, and were in Activity. "Do you think we should stop it at some point, or let them watch it right through?" "What would be an appropriate way to introduce the programme?" "Which of these interviews on the programme was the most harrowing for you, Sue?"

One evening in the group Sue lit a candle, placed it in the middle of the group, and suggested that they should have five minutes of silence, while each person thought about what that symbol meant for him or her. At the end, in a very slow and relaxed fashion, various members shared what they wanted to, of what had come up for them in the silence. It was a quiet, relaxed time, but it was Activity. It greatly helped the group to understand and accept each other.

5. Games

(see chapter 7)

As long as people have negative Life Positions, they will structure part of their time with Psychological Games in order to reinforce them. Games are exciting, and we seem to become addicted to certain ones. They provide lots of stroking, although most of it is experienced as negative for those involved. When Games are stopped, something that provides just as much stroking has to be put in their place. If not, the players will start up other Games to give the amount of stroking they each are used to receiving. Intimacy is the ideal replacement for Games.

6. Intimacy

Intimacy is used in T.A. terminology in a different way from its normal English usage.

In Intimacy, each person in the relationship is engaged in openly expressing his or her authentic feelings in an appropriate way. Each person is owning his or her own feelings, is not blaming the other for them, but is taking complete responsibility for feeling that way. In Games, there is an ulterior transaction - a "secret message" being sent at a different level from that of the words being said. In Intimacy, the words mean what they say. There is no ulterior message.

In Games, people are left with negative feelings which very often are carried over into another Game.

In Intimacy, feelings are expressed in such a way that they are out in the open and dealt with there and then. Jack and Sue sometimes fight. Recently they have been making a genuine effort to replace Games with Intimacy. Jack used to blame Sue for them taking the wrong path on the hills. He might say, "I felt you were probably going the wrong way when the path divided back there, but I didn't say anything, because I didn't want to start another row." Sue used to scream at Jack, "You make me feel so inadequate!"

Now Jack accepts the responsibility of telling Sue when he thinks she might be striding ahead on the wrong path, and of suggesting that they look at the map together. If she appears annoyed at this suggestion, he explains, "Sue, I need to know for myself. I'm feeling too tired today to take a wrong turning." Sue is now able to say, "When you called to me just now, I felt you were saying that I couldn't read a map properly. But my feeling comes from times when my father used to ridicule me in front of the rest of the family when I made a mistake. It's okay by me if we check up together."

One evening a new member came to the house group. He began to express opinions radically different from the ones normally expressed by the permanent members. The normal sense of togetherness and fellowship in the group was disrupted. Group members, unconscious of the rejecting hidden messages they were giving, began to gang up against him with remarks like "Of course, in this group we always do it this way," and to make remarks that referred back to incidents in the life of the group before the stranger came. They would not have dreamed of saying aloud to him, "You don't belong here," but eventually the new member said, "I'm feeling uncomfortable in this group. I came tonight because I've been feeling very lonely since I arrived in the district and the minister suggested I might come and get to know you all, but I think I'm maybe not right for this group." There was a stunned silence. The stranger had risked putting into words what they had experienced, but not voiced directly. What followed was a time of intimacy when various group members got in touch with their discounted feelings and owned them, and their guilt in playing Games to reject the new member.

To achieve Intimacy, all sorts of feelings need to be expressed directly - anger, guilt, love, fear, frustration, sadness and so on. These feelings need to be owned by the person who expresses them. "I feel ..." not "You made me feel..."

Eric Berne (1) believed that Intimacy is set up by the Adult ego-states of the parties involved, checking out mutual understanding of the contracts and commitments to each other. This gives the Child permission to relax and act freely and openly. The Parent ego-state can either help by its approval or wreck Intimacy by supplying critical comments in the inner dialogue.

Intimacy holds great risks of being rejected by another. The stroking is more intense than in any other way of time-structuring. Stewart and Joines (2) write: " Because intimacy is not preprogrammed, it is also the most unpredictable of all the ways of time-structuring. Thus from Child, I may perceive intimacy as being the most ' risky' way to relate to another person. Paradoxically, it is actually the least risky. When I and the other person are in intimacy, we are communicating without discounting."

It makes the one who initiates it very vulnerable. But when the other replies, being open and owning his or her feelings, the rewards in understanding, acceptance and trust can be enormous. Do we really need to try to protect ourselves by Games-playing?

In his epistles, John writes "There is no fear in love, perfect love drives out all fear." *I John 4:18a. Good News Bible.*

Surely this kind of intimacy should be experienced above all within a loving Christian fellowship.

1. Eric Berne: " Games People Play."
2. "T.A. Today" Ian Stewart and Vann Joines. Lifespace Publishing, Nottingham, England.

For you to think through by yourself, or with others.

1. How might you use this theory to structime time to give a variety of experience in Sunday morning worship, if you have a hand in preparing it?

2. Invite the participants in a group to write out two lists:

   a) 20 things they really love doing

   b) 20 things they remember doing in the past 24 hours.

   When they have completed their lists, ask them to decide which category of time-structuring each item comes under, and to put its initial beside it (eg "W" = Withdrawal).

   Now let them count up how many they have written in each category in each list, and then compare and contrast them.

   Finally, invite them to ask themselves the following questions, and to share their answers in the group if they wish.

   a) What, if anything, did I learn about my use of time?

   b) Am I happy with the way I structure my time?

   c) Do I want to make any changes?

3. Think through how the following might use all six ways of structuring time:

   a) prayer

   b) spending time with a friend

   c) a sexual relationship

4. If you play the Psychological Game of "Harried", think through carefully how this affects your total use of time.

    a)   Make a comparative diagram of it by drawing a circle like a clockface and dividing it up into the proportions you feel you give to each.

        eg

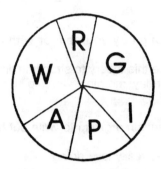

    b)   Now make another clock-face circle, but this time structure it to help you to stop needing to play "Harried" (ie you'll have to put something more exciting in its place!).

    c)   Share this with a friend and report to him or her in one week's time how you are managing to maintain change.

5. Recall three of the phrases you have used when you were angry and upset with a relative or friend. Write them down, then, opposite each, write down what you would say in their place, if you were to risk Intimacy.

    eg   "Look what you've made me do," becomes "I'm so angry with you that I've been careless and made a mistake."

CHAPTER 9

WHO ARE YOU? AND WHO CAN YOU BECOME?

Life script

*   Have you experienced someone growing up to be the kind of person you would expect to come from his particular family?

*   Have you noticed that some people seem to be always "winners" and others always "losers" in the game of life?

*   Are you just the same kind of person as you always seem to have been, or have you begun to change and grow and handle life much more lovingly and creatively than you ever did before?

What influences the kind of personality a person will choose to be?

All the bits and pieces of the theory of human personality fit into an overall pattern — a person's total response to life as he has so far experienced it and his plan for how he intends to be in the future — in Transactional Analysis terminology, his "LIFE SCRIPT".

What is life all about?

When a tiny helpless infant arrives in the setting prepared for him by those who have brought him into the world he has to set about almost immediately — and long before he is adequately equipped for such exploration — discovering for himself, the answers to the following questions: —

    1.   Who am I?
    2.   Who are all these other people?
    3.   What am I doing here?
    4.   What happens to someone like me?

His answers will be different from the answers discoverd by his siblings, his parents, his playmates, children born at the same time but of a different culture. . . and so on. Only HE will experience life from inside HIS skin. He will see an expression on his mother's face, and her reaction to a situation never seen by his older sister at his age because his mother has grown and changed through her experience of being a mother to his sister before him. He will experience life as an unique individual, and as that unique individual he will make his response to what happens to him.

Two girls in the same family can watch their mother trying to cope with a drinking problem. One can make the decision never to touch alcohol because of the effect her mother's drinking has had on the family: the other can look at her mother and decide that she is destined to become just like her, and can in fact become a problem drinker before she leaves school.

Two brothers can watch their dedicated clergy-man father, as they grow up. One can say to himself, "My father is loved and respected in this community. He's a person to whom others can turn. I want to be like him!" and that boy can dedicate himself to Christ and go into Christian social work. His brother can watch his father and say, "My father cares for everybody else, but when does he take me to a football match like Tom's father does?" He can decide that it'll be much more fun in life to be someone like Tom's father, and so turn away from the Christian life and accept other values for himself.

The answers to the basic questions of life come in various ways to the little person, but none come more forcibly than those she picks up from her parents. Parents pass on messages to their children about their expectations for them. Sometimes the messages are given quite deliberately and verbalised time and time again in the form of proverbs or slogans. "Satan finds some mischief for idle hands to do." "Waste not; want not." "You are the black sheep of the family." "Go away and don't bother me." "I love you." "All my troubles began the day you were born." "You were a long time coming, but you were worth waiting for."

When the little person hears these sayings he comes to his own conclusions as to what they say about him and usually he decides to act on what he has heard. Messages are sent and received about every area of what it means to be a person living amongst other people — messages about sexuality, money, learning, appearance, work, play, religion, and so on. Sometimes contrasting messages will be given by the mother and the father, or by the parents and the grandparents. Messages can come through any emotionally significant person throughout the growing years. The little person will have to decide which messages are the ones he should obey, or decide on ambivalence.

64

Some messages convey major themes for the pattern of the little person's life, such as 'black sheep' , ' someone who always brings trouble' , ' just like your Aunt Matilda', ' a born teacher', and these themes will affect many if not all aspects of her personality.

Other messages are more limited and affect only certain areas, for example, her attitude to money and other material possessions. Some can contribute to obvious discrepancies in a person's life-style, such as being highly organised and efficient in the work situation and in perpetual chaos at home.

Up to the age of about five or six, a little child lives in a world where fantasy and reality are hard for her to separate. Witches and Dr. Who, baby Moses and the lost sheep, dreams and magic spells can be as vivid to her as an aunt who lives in another town or an event which actually happened yesterday. The death of a pet, the arrival of a new baby, or her mother's sudden anger, can be as mysterious to her as the antics on a cartoon she may watch on T.V. It is while she views life like this that the beginnings of her life script are in formation.

In answer to the big questions of life like "Who am I? she will sometimes hear a fairy tale, or see a film, or look at a picture on the wall, or be told a Bible story and say to herself, "That is about someone just like me." In fact, all through our lives, certain novels, certain films, and certain Bible stories have an emotional impact on us far beyond the effect they have on a friend to whom we may recommend them. This is because we have identified with one of the characters. It's a story about someone "just like me." If a little girl, for example, identifies with Cinderella, then she discovers the answer to the question, "What happens to someone like me?" It may seem odd, but this kind of discovery can still influence that little girl when she is a grown woman and has to relate to an authoritarian woman at work, or when she finds herself competing with "the Ugly Sisters"!

And so, very early in life, a person decides his answers to the four basic questions and these form the basis of what he sets out to become. He writes a life script from which he acts, choosing to relate to the complementary characters he meets along the way, and so long as he follows his script, he feels he can cope.

Transactional Analysis outlines three main types of Life Scripts — a CONSTRUCTIVE or WINNING SCRIPT, a 'GOING NOWHERE' SCRIPT and a DESTRUCTIVE or LOSING SCRIPT.

Awareness of this, and of the various aspects of this theory of personality that go to make up the Life Script theme, opens up choices for people who have Going Nowhere, or Destructive Scripts to change to the Constructive or Winning Script.

The Script in each person's life contains together positive and negative elements which have developed side by side. The balance of this can be changed.

Because the Life Script is based upon decisions taken in early childhood when the little person came to conclusions about himself and other people before he had sufficient experience in life to make a balanced judgement, the Script can be re-examined in grown-up life by the Adult ego state together with a much wiser Parent ego state than was available to a three year old, and new decisions can be made in the Child ego state to change from destructive or going nowhere patterns to a Winning Script.

Decision, renewal, conversion are words, experiences and action which describe response to just such a liberating power, releasing constructive energy for living.

Jesus Christ is, for Christians, the source and focus of that power. Through him and through his affirmation of us, we may take courage to break our Script and discover for ourselves the truth of the experience he offers, "I make all things new."

It is true of the Church as of any other community that it will express both negative and positive life styles. As it is increasingly open to his Spirit, so men and women will know the truth that will set them free.

Most people seem to want to change. Most are aware of aspects of their personalities that war against loving open relationships with other people, and even against their own ability to accept themselves as lovable.

Jesus Christ can effect change in our personalities. He can do this almost in spite of us, or he can do it with our co-operation and determination to be different.

There is a parallel here to physical healing. Sometimes the Spirit works miraculously and instantaneously in a person's body, bringing healing beyond the powers of our medical knowledge to date. Most often, though, he chooses to use modern drugs, surgery, nursing skills or alternative therapies alongside a patient's will to get better to bring about the healing of the body.

In the healing of our personalities, Transactional Analysis is one of the tools we believe his Spirit uses, especially within the context of the Christian community to urge us towards change and renewal that we might become the loving people who can work together for his Kingdom coming.

For you to think through for yourself, or with others.

1. a) Make a list of five stories in the Bible which have an emotional impact on you when you read them.

   b) Now ask yourself: "Are any of these stories about 'someone like me'?".

2. Which was your favourite fairy-tale as a child? (If none comes to mind, then perhaps you will remember a comic-strip character, a TV series, a story you read for yourself in Primary School, a Bible Story you loved as a child, a film you were taken to see, a picture which hung on your bedroom wall, etc.)

   When you think of it now, can you imagine it helping you to answer any of the following questions for you in your early years?

   a) Who am I?
   b) Who are all these other people?
   c) What am I doing here?
   d) What happens to someone like me?

3. Draw a map of your life's journey until now, marking each experience when something happened to set free some of the potential inside you that hadn't had a chance to develop before then.

   Then make a fantasy projection of your journey from now on as you would like it to be with your as-yet-untapped potential having an opportunity to grow and flower.

4. If your favourite fairy-tale or other story when you were a child seems to have had a significant effect on the pattern of your life so far, think it through carefully.

Take some time by yourself and write it out as completely as you can from memory as if it was happening to you now — so use the first person and the present tense, and write from the point of view of the character you identify with most.

After that, rewrite it, taking out all the parts you decide you no longer want and substituting some other way of working out the plot.

Then ask yourself: "What will I need to do now to make sure my life follows the positive and not the negative plot?".

5. Take a Biblical character whose life changed dramatically for good — eg Zacchaeus, Mary Magdalene, Saul/Paul, Simon Peter — and examine the records to discover in which ways they changed and in which ways they remained the same.

(For example, when Saul changed to become Paul he still had the same tremendous zeal and energy, he still travelled from city to city, he was still a leader amongst his fellow men, but his hatred had changed to love.)

As far as Christians are concerned, Jesus is the Script-breaker, so, after this Bible Study, ask yourself: "Which specific personality trait in me would I love to have changed to the exact opposite?". It is one of the good gifts your heavenly Father wants to give to you, so

a) pray for it

b) begin to live as if your prayer has been answered

c) ask a group or a friend to pray for you too and to tell you when there is any change in your behaviour.

BOOKS FOR FURTHER READING

"Born to Win"   M. James and D. Jongeward   Signet Books

This is an excellent book for those who want a readable but very thorough look at T.A. It contains many suggestions for individuals and groups to explore to get to know themselves and each other better.

"Finding Hidden Treasure"   Lura Jane Geiger   Jalmar Press, Inc.

This is a book full of good suggestions for any who wish to teach T.A. to groups in the church.

"Marriage is for Loving"   M. James   Addison-Wesley

A beautiful and most helpful book for all Christian couples — and for those who want their marriage to be more loving, yet who wouldn't call themselves Christian. An excellent book for those involved in helping others to deepen their marriage relationships.

"A Tool for Christians" (Book Two)   Jean C. Morrison (Grigor)
                Church of Scotland Department of Education

A further book which teaches the use of Transactional Analysis to encourage growth in loving relationships within the Christian community.

"T.A. Today"   Stewart and Joines   Lifespan 1987